JOKES THAT STINK!

AND OTHER GROSS FACTS

BLUE
BIKE
BOOKS

Ashley Bilodeau

Contents

2

Fart Poetry

A fart can be quiet
A fart can be loud
Some leave a powerful
Poisonous cloud

Some farts do not smell
While others are vile
A fart may pass quickly
Or linger awhile

A fart can be
Short, or a fart
Can be long
Some farts have been
Known to sound just
Like a song

A fart can create
A most-curious medley
A fart can be harmless
Or silent, but deadly

A fart can occur
In a number of places
And leave everyone
With strange looks
On their faces

From wide-open prairies
To small elevators
A fart will find all of us
Sooner or later

So be not afraid
Of the invisible gas
For always remember
That farts, too, shall pass.

Farts in Rhyme!

She who observed it, served it.

He who declared it, blared it.

The next person who speaks is the person who reeks.

He who detected it, ejected it.

Farts in Rhyme!

Whoever asked, gassed.

Whoever denied it, supplied it.

The smeller's the feller.

8

Fart Jokes

What do you call someone who refuses to fart in public? **A private tooter!**

What do you get when the Queen farts? **A noble gas!**

Why are ninja farts so dangerous? **They're silent but deadly!**

How do you make regular baths into bubble baths? **Eat beans for dinner!**

What is the smelliest breakfast cereal? **Toot Loops!**

11

Fart Jokes

What happened to the man who only ate Skittles? **He farted rainbows!**

How can you tell when a clown just farted? **It smells funny!**

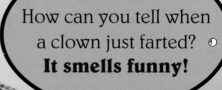

What do you get when you mix
a brain and a fart together?
A brain fart!

What's gross?
**Farting in
the bathtub.**

What's grosser?
**Catching the
bubble with
your teeth!**

When should
you stop telling
fart jokes?
**When everyone
says you stink!**

13

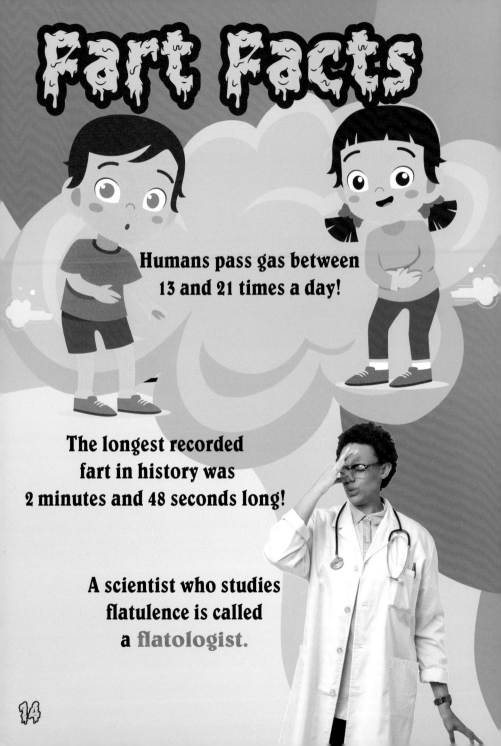

Farts travel about 10 feet (3 meters) per second!

The oldest recorded joke is an ancient fart joke that dates back to 1900

15

Poop Jokes

Are you ready for a poop joke?

No, they stink!

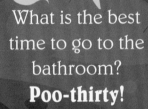

What is the best time to go to the bathroom? **Poo-thirty!**

What do you call a 12-inch stool? **A footstool!**

16

What did the turd say to the butt? **I don't ever want to go through that again!**

What's brown and sticky? **A stick!**

What did the poop say to the fart? **You blow me away!**

Poop Facts

The healthiest poop is a long log that comes out in one piece and that sinks to the bottom of the toilet.

THERE ARE SEVEN TYPES OF POOP!

 Separate hard lumps (like nuts)

 Sausage-shaped (lumpy)

 Like a sausage but with cracks on the surface

 Like a sausage or snake (smooth and soft)

 Soft blobs with clear-cut edges

 Fluffy pieces with ragged edges (mushy)

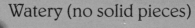 Watery (no solid pieces)

George Frandsen

The largest
collection of fossilized poops
is made up of 1277 prehistoric poops!

Poop is 75% water!

19

Toilet Jokes

What did the sink say to the potty?

You look flushed!

Why did the toilet paper roll down the hill?
To get to the bottom!

Why can't you hear a pterodactyl go to the bathroom?
Because the "P" is silent!

Why didn't the toilet paper make it across the road?

It got stuck in the crack!

Toilet Jokes

There are two reasons you shouldn't drink from the toilet. **Number 1 and number 2!**

Why were there balloons in the bathroom? **There was a birthday potty!**

Other Names

For the Toilet

What names can you think of for this toilet?

Throne Room

Water Closet
Washroom
Garderobe
Restroom
OUTHOUSE
Lavatory
FACILITY
Latrine
Powder Room
Throne Room
Cloakroom
JOHN
KHAZI
Dunny
Bog Can
Privy
Potty

What other names for the toilet can you come up with?

What does
a cloud wear under
its raincoat?
Thunderwear!

Why does a pirate
wear underwear?
To hide his booty!

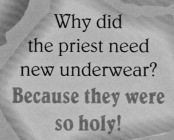

Why did
the priest need
new underwear?
**Because they were
so holy!**

What did the dog say when he was sick?

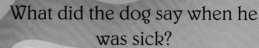

BARF

BARF

What do you call it when you barf while laughing?
Upchuckle!

What is food backwards?
Barf!

Did you hear about the guy who vomited while sky diving?
It's all over town!

What's gross?
A cat barfing all over the floor.
What's grosser?
Another cat eating it up!

28

Barf Jokes

OTHER WORDS FOR BARFING

PUKING

PROJECTILING

Yakking

RALPHING

Screaming cookies

Making gut soup

hurling

Upchucking

Retching

Tossing your cookies

Losing your lunch

Vomiting

Burp Jokes

What colour
is a belch?
Burple!

What does the Queen
do when she burps?
**She issues
a royal pardon.**

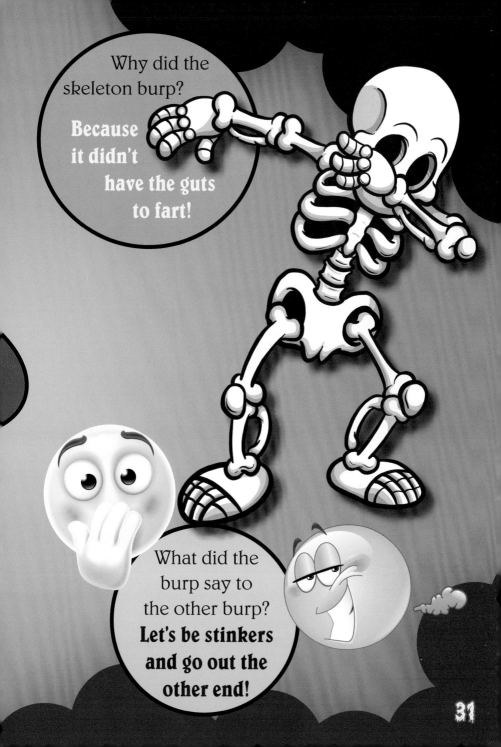

Booger Jokes

What monster sits on the tip of your finger?
The boogeyman!

What's the difference between boogers and broccoli?
Kids don't eat broccoli!

Booger Facts

How do you make a hankie dance? **You put a little boogie in it!**

What do you get when a dinosaur blows its nose? **Out of the way!**

36

Booger Facts

Boogers are a chunky piece of dried mucus from your nose.

You might have heard a booger called snot.

Boogers can be wet, dry, bendy, crunchy or stringy!

The world record for longest nails is 42 feet 10 inches (13.06 meters) long!

GUINNESS WORLD RECORDS™

Diana Armstrong

Gross World Records

More Gross World Records

The longest ear hairs in the world are 9 inches (25 centimeters) long!

The record for the longest mustache in the world is 14 feet (4.3 meters)!

Ram Singh Chauhan

What's gross? **Finding a hair in your food.**

What's grosser? **Finding out it's your grandma's nose hair!**

49

What do you call a cat who likes to eat beans? **Puss n' Toots!**

Why do ducks have tail feathers? **To cover their buttquacks!**

What's gross? **When a dog digs in the litter box for kitty poops.**

What's grosser? **When the dog licks its owner after!**

Gross Animal Jokes

What is
invisible and
smells like carrots?
Rabbit farts!

Why did the
chicken cross
the road?
**The chicken next
to her farted.**

51

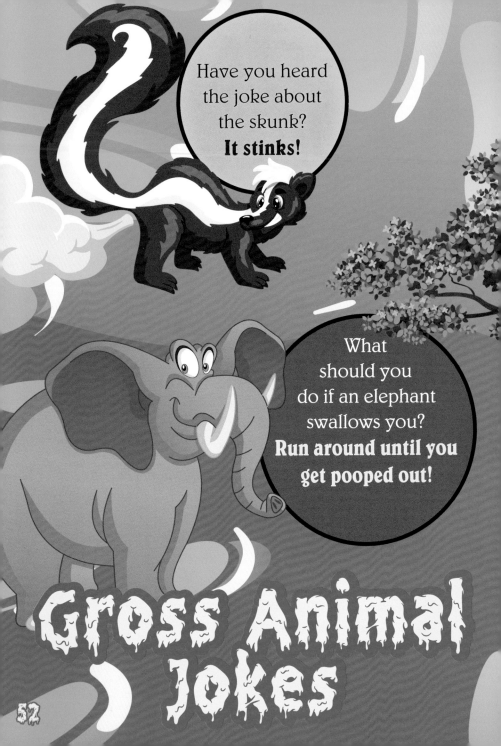

Gross Animal Jokes

Did you know?
Panda bears poop 40 times a day!

How did the
yeti feel when he
had the flu?
Abominable.

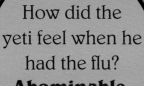

What do you call a dinosaur that doesn't take a bath?
A stink-o-saurus!

Why are dinosaurs no longer around?
Because their eggs stink!

Gross Dinosaur Jokes

Creepy Crawly Jokes

What is a spider's favorite event? **Webbings!**

What do spiders order at restaurants? **Burgers and flies!**

Gross Monsters!

Why didn't the skeleton cross the road? **It had no guts!**

Why don't vampires sneeze? **Because they're too busy coffin.**

Gross Monsters!

Why didn't the skeleton cross the road? **It had no guts!**

Why don't vampires sneeze? **Because they're too busy coffin.**

What do you call a fairy that doesn't like to shower? **Stinkerbell.**

What is smelly and strong? **Cheese!**

The Publisher: Blue Bilke Books

Library and Archives Canada Cataloguing in Publication

Title: Jokes that stink! : and other gross facts / Ashley Bilodeau.

Names: Bilodeau, Ashley, 1995– author.

Identifiers: Canadiana (print) 20220402752 | Canadiana (ebook) 20220402795 | ISBN 9781989209387 (softcover) | ISBN 9781989209394 (PDF)

Subjects: LCSH: Wit and humor, Juvenile. | LCSH: Gastrointestinal gas—Juvenile humor. | LCSH: Gastrointestinal gas—Miscellanea—Juvenile literature. | LCGFT: Humor.

Classification: LCC PN6178.C3 B55 2023 | DDC jC818/.602—dc23

Front cover: From Getty Images-AaronAmat; HADIIA POLIASHENKO; lineartestpilot; S-S-S.

Back cover: From Getty Images-rexcanor; lineartestpilot.

Photo credits: From Getty Images,-ALINA-, 36; Aaron_Wardell, 32; AaronAmat, 14, 16; ACarnography, 54; Allevinatis, 38; Alyona Jitnaya, 2, 16, 17; angkritth, 28; ankomando, 28; AnnaViolet, 16; arryrains, 41; Aryo Hadi, 39; BabySofja, 19; bayuprahara, 59; bennyb, 3, 16, 17; Best Content Production Group, 23; lueringmedia, 57; bokan76, 7; Carol Hamilton, 51; Chemlamp, 23; ChrisGorgio, 6, 30, 31; Christopher Robbins, 48; Colorfuel Studio, 14; Darko Mlinarevic, 60; Dave Matchett, 50; DeluXe-PiX, 28; denis_pc, 52; DeShoff, 56; drogatnev zesaiphio 20, dvulikaia, 56; ericb007, 2, 28, 29; Flickr Daniel Throne Toilet, 24;Gorrilar_Vector, 53; Guiness logo, 19, 46, 47, 49; hermandesign2015, 59; ia_64, 37; Igor Petrovic, 17, 19; Igor Zakowski, 40, 54; Ilya Okty Zesaiphio, 58; insemar, 27; intararit, 35; Irina Cheremisinova, 62; IRYNA NASKOVA, 18, 59; Iuliia Kanivets, 15; JFLangton, 17; jgroup, 15; Jrcasas, 13; julos, 53; June Jacobsen, 45; K_Thalhofer, 22; KanKhem, 27; kellykellykelly, 39; klyaksun, 42; Koldunova_Anna, 12; KOSON, 57; Kukurund, 15; Lexi Claus, 26; lineartestpilot, 2, 3, 29, 32, 33, 35, 33; Liudmila Baskelovich blue, 41,43, 44; MartinLisner, 24; master1305, 44; memoangeles, 31, 34, 61; Mironov Konstantin, 41; nicoletaionescu, 37; Nohan Budiono, 7; Nohan Budiono, 9; ogieurvil, 4; Pedro Fernandes, 20, 22; Pramote Lertnitivanit, 4; PrettyVectors, 40; Refluo, 55; rexcanor, 11, ridjam; 44, Roi and Roi, 61; S-S-S, 4, 5, 6, 9, 30, 63; Salman Alfa, 14; Samuil_Levich, 5, 39, 55; schulzie, 50; seamartini, 61; sebastian coll, 42; Sebastian Gorczowski, 25; Sevulya, 51; shock77, 38; siraanamwong, 21; Smokeyjo, 36; SurfUpVector, 38; Suzi Media Production, 34; Tamara Antipina, 52; Tigatelu, 21, 60, 50; Tomacco, 63; TopVectors, 49; VikiVector, 26; Voyagerix, 63; Voysla, 2; Voysla, 35; XtockImages, 38; yayayoyo, 5, 9, 31; Yevhen Cherkasov, 62; Ysr Dora, 3, Ysr Dora, 28; Yuri_Arcurs, 30; Yurich84, 8.

We acknowledge the financial support of the Government of Canada.
Nous reconnaissons l'appui financier du gouvernement du Canada.

Funded by the   Financé par le
Government   gouvernement
of Canada   du Canada

Canadä

Produced with the assistance of the Government of Alberta. *Alberta*

Printed in China
PC: 38-1